Tractor Ted

TED 1

Activity Book

1 Excavator

one

2 Harvesters

Two

3 Combines

Three

4 Kittens

four

5 Piglets

five

6 Bales

six

7 Chickens

Seven

8 Goats

eight

9 Cows

Nina

Match these fields with the machine

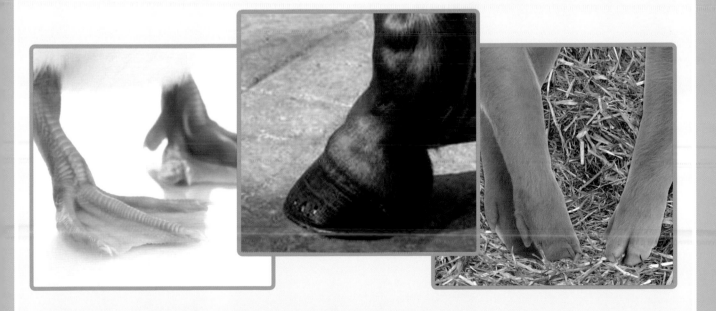

Match the mother to the baby

Match these vehicles with their trailer

I hope you had fun matching

Woof!

Spot the 5 differences

Spot the 4 differences

Could you
spot them?

TED 1

Which of these is the odd one out?

Which of these is the odd one out?

Did you find them?

TED 1

Big

Small

In

Out

Up

Down

Hot

Cold

Can you think of any more?

TED 1

Tractor Wheel Sandwiches

Ingredients
- Sliced bread with crusts removed
- Various sandwich fillings.
  Filling ideas:
  - Cheese spread and wafer thin ham
  - Tuna mayonnaise
  - Chocolate spread (for muddy looking wheels)

Method
- Cut the crusts off medium sliced bread and press each slice lightly with a rolling pin.
- Spread with favourite fillings.
- Roll up as a swiss roll and cut into slices.

Carrot Cake

Ingredients
- 170g Light brown sugar • 3 large eggs, lightly beaten
- 170g Margarine or Butter • 170g grated carrot • 2 chopped ripe bananas • 285g self-raising flour • 1 tsp bicarbonate of soda
- 2 tsp Baking Powder • 170g Cream cheese • 115g icing sugar
- ½ tsp Vanilla Essence

Method
- Preheat the oven to 160C.
- Grease & line a 30cm by 20cm tin.
- Put the sugar, eggs, flour, margarine, bicarb & baking powder into mixer & beat together
- Peel and grate carrots & chop bananas into small pieces
- Add carrot & chopped banana to mixture & mix together
- Put into prepared cake tin
- Cook in the oven for 50-60 minutes